MONUMENTAL
GREAT EVENTS

D1266441

The Story of the Underground Railroad

Africans, many of whom had never seen ships, were forced into the lower levels of ships bound for the New World.

Mitchell Lane

PUBLISHERS
P.O. Box 196
Hockessin, Delaware 19707

Titles in the Series

MONUMENTAL MILESTONES
GREAT EVENTS OF MODERN TIMES

The Story of the Underground Railroad

Harriet Tubman (far left) was enslaved in Maryland. After her own escape in 1849, she spent more than ten years trying to rescue her family and friends.

KaaVonia Hinton

Mitchell Lane
PUBLISHERS

Printing   1   2   3   4   5   6   7   8   9

Library of Congress Cataloging-in-Publication Data
Hinton, KaaVonia, 1973–
  The story of the Underground Railroad / by KaaVonia Hinton.
      p. cm. — (Monumental milestones)
  Includes bibliographical references and index.
  ISBN 978-1-58415-739-7 (library bound)
  1. Underground Railroad—Juvenile literature. 2. Fugitive slaves—United States—History—19th century—Juvenile literature. 3. Antislavery movements—United States—History—19th century—Juvenile literature. 4. Abolitionists—United States—History—19th century—Juvenile literature. I. Title.
  E450.H634 2010
  973.7'115—dc22
                                                            2009027367

ABOUT THE AUTHOR: KaaVonia Hinton is an assistant professor in the Teaching & Learning department at Old Dominion University in Norfolk, Virginia. She is the author of *Angela Johnson: Poetic Prose* (Scarecrow Press), *Sharon M. Draper: Embracing Literacy* (Scarecrow Press) and, for Mitchell Lane Publishers, *Jacqueline Woodson* and *Desegregating America's Schools*.

PUBLISHER'S NOTE: This story is based on the author's extensive research, which she believes to be accurate. Documentation of such research is contained on page 45.

The internet sites referenced herein were active as of the publication date. Due to the fleeting nature of some web sites, we cannot guarantee they will all be active when you are reading this book.

Contents

*For Your Information

Harriet Tubman leading fugitive slaves through the woods

Though Tubman was petite, she was strong and brave. She carried a gun to protect freedom seekers. She often boasted that she never lost a passenger while working on the Underground Railroad.

Running on the Railroad

No one really knows when the Underground Railroad began aiding enslaved people on their quest for freedom. Some researchers say it began in 1804 when a man named General Thomas Boudes of Columbia, Pennsylvania, hid a fugitive slave and refused to give her up to law enforcers. Others say the organization began much later, in 1830 or 1831, when an enslaved man named Tice Davids escaped his owner's Kentucky plantation. Tice ran and jumped in the Ohio River before his owner could stop him. Swimming as fast as he could, Tice made it to shore in Ripley, Ohio, just moments before his owner's boat reached the Ohio side of the river. But when Tice's owner looked for him, all traces of the runaway had disappeared. When the owner retold the story to others, he said that Tice "must have gone off on an underground road."[1]

The term *underground road* was revised to *Underground Railroad* after the invention of steam railroads in 1830. Trains fascinated Americans, so people who helped escaped slaves decided to use railroad terms to secretly describe their work. The "Underground Railroad" was a group of people, safe houses, and hiding places that helped runaway slaves escape to freedom. A "passenger" or "package" was a fugitive slave in need of assistance from an "agent," a person who knew the routes escaped slaves should take. A "depot" or "station" was where an escaped slave could find help. Stations were houses, churches, and businesses. Escapees also met "conductors" who helped them get to the next safe place. Escape routes led to the North, even into Canada; south into Mexico and the Caribbean; and west beyond the borders of the Union.

Many enslaved people learned about the Underground Railroad from conductors. Some conductors from the North went south to tell enslaved people about it. People all across the country worked on the Underground Railroad.

For example, after his escape from a plantation in Maryland, Frederick Douglass began speaking out against slavery and eventually began hiding escapees in his home in Rochester, New York.

The town in which Tice Davids went "underground"—Ripley, Ohio—was known for having citizens who were dedicated to helping escaped slaves, such as John Rankin, a local minister, and John Parker, a free black man. A few years after John Parker bought his freedom in 1845, he began traveling to the border of Kentucky, a slave state, to look for enslaved people who wanted to cross the Ohio River on their way to freedom. Once he helped them across, he showed them how to get to the next station, usually John Rankin's house, where Rankin's wife and thirteen children welcomed them with food and clothes. Parker helped at least one escapee a week across the river.[2]

Cincinnati, Ohio, also had a number of citizens devoted to the Underground Railroad. In fact, it was the home of Levi Coffin, the man known as the president of the Underground Railroad. Coffin and his wife, Catherine, helped thousands of escapees, hiding them in secret places throughout their home.[3]

By helping freedom seekers, conductors and agents were breaking the law. They risked being arrested, jailed, and fined. Historian James O. Horton writes, "It was dangerous to be involved with the Underground Railroad no matter what color you were. There were white people who spent years of their lives in jail."[4]

In 1848, Thomas Garrett, an abolitionist in Delaware, was convicted of helping enslaved people hide, disguise themselves, and find transportation. Being punished for breaking the law did not stop him. Moments after hearing how he would be punished, he said he would continue to give food, money, clothes, and shelter to help slaves obtain freedom. Many of the slaves Garrett helped were sent on to the Antislavery Office in Philadelphia. Some of the slaves he helped get to Philadelphia were escorted by Harriet Tubman, a freedom seeker who escaped to Pennsylvania in 1849. After escaping from Maryland, she traveled back South numerous times to help others obtain freedom. Once in Philadelphia, Tubman usually took the freedom seekers to the Pennsylvania Society for the Abolition of Slavery, where William Still, a free black man who helped about sixty fugitive slaves a month travel along the Underground Railroad, was waiting.[5]

The freedom seeker was also breaking the law, so the work of the Underground Railroad had to be secret. Most information about escaping had to be memorized. According to historians Jacqueline Tobin and Raymond G. Dobard, it was "passed on only by word of mouth, using codes, signs, and signals created by slaves and shared only with those who could be trusted."[6] Sometimes the conductor and passengers used a hoot-owl sound to communicate at night; at other times, they used secret knocks and coded notes. In August 1843, for example, John Stone of Belpre, Ohio, sent a note with codes in it to David Putnam. The note read, "Business is arranged for Saturday night be on the lookout and if practicable let a carriage come & meet the carawan [caravan] JS."[7]

According to historian J. Blaine Hudson, in the beginning, escapees were mostly young men who escaped "in reaction to or to avoid brutality, sexual exploitation, separation from family—and in response to broken promises, or simply because freedom beckoned."[8] Later, once the Underground Railroad

The Underground Railroad, painted in 1893 by Charles T. Webber. The painting shows leading abolitionists in Cincinnati, Ohio—Levi Coffin, the "president" of the Underground Railroad; his wife, Catherine; and Hannah Haydock—helping a family find freedom in the North.

became more organized and talked about, women and children began to run away more often. Sometimes entire families sought freedom together. It is believed that Harriet Tubman made nineteen trips as a conductor. Some of the 300 people she led to freedom were family members. In 1857, she helped her parents escape. They were too old to walk, so she drove them through the woods in a wagon.

No one really knows how many slaves actually found freedom through the Underground Railroad. However, scholars estimate that the total number of enslaved people who traveled through Philadelphia alone during the colonial period and the antebellum period, the period before the Civil War, was probably more than 9,000. The total number of escapees who made it to a free state in the North or to Canada is estimated to be between 20,000 and 100,000.[9]

Running away was dangerous and the punishment was severe. Slave catchers or hunters made their living locating and returning runaway slaves. Runaway slaves generally traveled at night because they did not want to be discovered. They often used the North Star to direct them north. During the day, they hid wherever they could.

The routes changed over time, so freedom seekers took different routes throughout the years. Escapees went through small towns and large cities while traveling on the Underground Railroad. They were also likely to travel over rivers, valleys, and mountains to get to a station.

When conductors carried escapees to the next safe house, escapees sometimes hid under fruits and vegetables on wagons. The stations were usually ten to twenty miles apart, just close enough so that a person on foot, or someone in a wagon, could cover the distance in one night. Once at the safe house, an escaped slave might hide in a cellar or attic, or behind a trapdoor. The freedom seeker would stay in one safe house for a while and then move on until he or she finally made it to a place where freedom was possible.

Home of Levi Coffin, a stop on the Underground Railroad

Traveling and working on the Underground Railroad was against the law, and it was dangerous. Enslaved people and their friends on the Underground Railroad had to make sure no one knew they were involved in an illegal plan to help enslaved people leave their owners. Fearing punishment for their crime, they created secret signals, passwords, and codes so that they could communicate with each other without anyone else understanding. Scholars say the secret signals of the Underground Railroad probably had different meanings in every community. Enslaved people and their friends used dances, birdcalls, knocks, notes, handshakes, and lights in windows to transmit messages.

Well-known songs and quilts contained signals, too. Enslaved people changed the words in some hymns, or religious songs, to communicate secretly with each other. Songs such as "Follow the Drinking Gourd," "Wade in the Water," and "Steal Away" secretly communicated ideas about escaping. (The "drinking gourd" refers to the Big Dipper, which points the way north.)

Some researchers believe that quilts with African symbols on them told enslaved people how to travel to freedom. Others say the quilts did not have messages on them, but the act of hanging a quilt outside one's home was a signal to escaped slaves that it was safe to ask the people in the home for help. The ceramic figure of a black man holding a lantern, a lawn jockey, was used in a similar way. If someone's yard had a lawn jockey on it, an escaped slave would suspect that the person was a helpful friend. The placement of the lantern in the jockey's hand, or a ribbon tied to it, were further messages (green for safe, red for danger). These signals and secret codes helped keep escapees safe on their journey on the Underground Railroad.

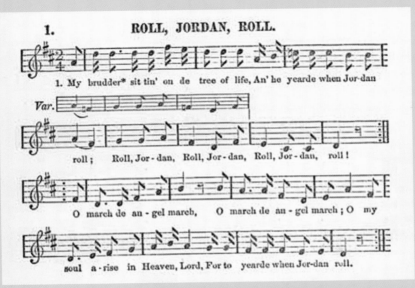

Slaves sang songs like "Roll, Jordan, Roll" to communicate with each other.

After a long journey on a Dutch s
Africans arrived at Jamestown in 161

Historians believe the Africans were from Angola. Some say the Africans were not slaves because the Virginia census of 1623 and 1624 listed them as servants.

A Slave for Life

Harriet Tubman, Frederick Douglass, and Thomas Garrett are just a few of the well-known workers on the Underground Railroad. But the foundation of the Underground Railroad was laid before these individuals were born. It started when the African slave trade brought captives to the Western Hemisphere. As historian Karen James says, "The Underground Railroad is not about trapdoors or hidden tunnels or secret compartments. It's about the struggle to end slavery and how basic, ordinary people did extraordinary things when faced with human need."[1]

The first Africans to arrive in the British colonies came to Virginia, near present-day Hampton, in August 1619. There were about twenty of them, and it is believed that the ship's captain had taken the Africans from a Spanish ship. The captain, hungry and worn, gave the Africans to Jamestown colonists in exchange for food. Sources say that these Africans were not slaves. They were treated as indentured servants, forced to work for the colonists for a number of years before being set free.

Virginians were eager to build homes, clear and prepare land for planting crops, and make a comfortable living for themselves. At first the settlers were not too particular about who helped them. They enslaved Native Americans and employed black and white indentured servants. Many of the whites sold themselves into contract slavery in return for passage to America, but other white indentured servants were kidnapped and taken to the colonies to work.[2] White indentured servants were often young, poor, in trouble with the law, or debtors (people who owed a significant amount of money to someone). Used in Virginia, Maryland, and the Carolinas, they were generally inexpensive and easy to obtain. Just like black indentured servants, white indentured servants could be sold and punished, but they would eventually be freed.

In 1640, three indentured servants escaped from a farm in Virginia. Two of them, Victor and James Gregory, were white, and the other one, John Punch, was black. They reached Maryland, but were eventually caught, tried, and convicted of running away. Though each man's crime was the same, their sentences were not equal. Punishment for Victor and James consisted of additional years in servitude, while John was sentenced to life in servitude. This case marked a turning point in using Africans as slaves. By 1685, the use of white indentured servants had decreased, and so had the use of black indentured servants. Most blacks had become slaves for life.

Africans were probably chosen for several reasons: they were strong, inexpensive, and highly visible. A minority in most areas, Africans easily stood out among the white majority. The colonists might have also chosen to enslave Africans because they were unprotected—meaning they did not enjoy the protection of recognized governments such as Britain and Ireland, as whites did.[3] Why didn't the colonists enslave more Native Americans? Many Native

Enslaved people were forced to wear spurs, iron collars, leg irons, and masks so that owners could easily control them. Shackles were used when slaves were forced to walk long distances and when they were transported in ships.

Shackles made it difficult for enslaved people to run away.

Americans died from European diseases, and others were able to resist enslavement, so the colonists depended mainly on Africans.

Virginia, Maryland, and New York led the way in declaring Africans as slaves for life. Virginia even decided the fate of black children by establishing a rule that said children would be enslaved or free depending on the mother's status. If the mother was a slave, the child would be considered a slave.

Different people all over the world have enslaved others for different reasons. In Africa, for example, people were made slaves when they committed crimes or were captured in war. However, slaves in Africa usually retained some rights, and they were released from slavery after working for a certain amount of time.

Slave traders found various ways of taking Africans from their homes. Some African kings traded their citizens to slavers for weapons and other goods. Slave hunters kidnapped other Africans. Olaudah Equiano was kidnapped from his village in Nigeria (Benin) in the 1750s, when he was about eleven years old. In 1789, he published an autobiography titled *The Interesting Narrative of the Life of Olaudah Equiano, or Gustavus Vassa, the African.* He wrote:

> . . . some of us [children] used to get up a tree to look out for any . . . kidnapper that might come upon us—for they sometimes took those opportunities of our parents' absence, to attack and carry off as many as they could. . . . One day as I was watching, . . . I saw one of those people come into the yard of our neighbor . . . to kidnap. . . . I gave the alarm."[4]

After Equiano sounded the alarm, the children managed to tie the kidnapper up until their parents arrived. They were saved on that day, but on another, two men and a woman managed to capture Equiano and his sister. Later, Equiano worked as the servant of a British naval officer and eventually obtained his freedom. He never saw his sister again.

Slave hunters would also attack entire villages, capturing those who remained alive after the battle. Captured slaves were often chained together and marched for miles to the coast of Africa, where they were forced onto ships. Africans were tightly packed into these ships. They had little room to move

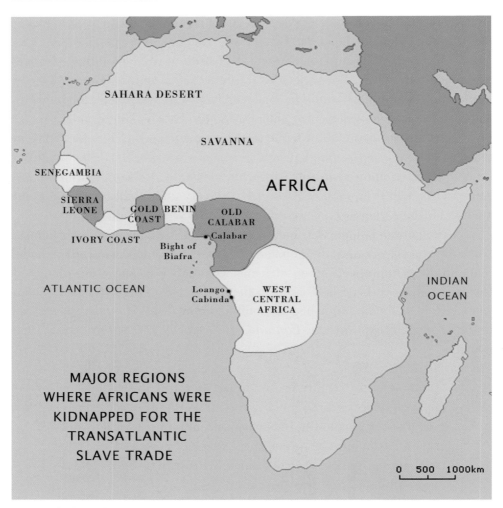

SAHARA DESERT

SAVANNA

SENEGAMBIA

AFRICA

SIERRA LEONE

GOLD COAST

BENIN

OLD CALABAR

•Calabar

IVORY COAST

Bight of Biafra

ATLANTIC OCEAN

Loango•
Cabinda•

WEST CENTRAL AFRICA

INDIAN OCEAN

MAJOR REGIONS
WHERE AFRICANS WERE
KIDNAPPED FOR THE
TRANSATLANTIC
SLAVE TRADE

0   500   1000km

Most of the Africans were captured from the West Coast and then forced to march hundreds of miles to the Ivory Coast. Once there, they were examined and loaded onto ships in preparation for the Middle Passage across the Atlantic Ocean. The long, dangerous voyage took six to ten weeks. Many enslaved people did not survive the trip.

about and no privacy at all, as they were chained to at least one other person. They were given very little food or exercise, and many were forced to use the bathroom wherever they could. Some Africans died of such diseases as smallpox and dysentery, while others died of starvation.

Once enslaved Africans reached the colonies, they were sold. Slave owners and traders did not view slaves as human beings, so they did not think selling slaves was wrong. They also did not think it was wrong to hurt them physically or separate them from family and friends. Africans spoke a large number of different languages, so sometimes it was hard to communicate with each other and with owners. Africans who might have been from the same or neighboring tribes were often separated. Initially, this made it difficult for them to bond and make sense of what was happening to them.

Slaves in the South usually lived on farms. Small farms had less than twenty slaves, while larger farms, or plantations, could have over one hundred. According to historian Susan Altman, the slaves on large plantations were often "divided into three groups: field hands, house slaves and those with particular skills, such as blacksmiths, drivers, or carpenters."[5] They were forced to work in fields that grew crops such as tobacco, sugar, rice, and cotton. The more the enslaved people worked, the richer their owners became. In the North, winters

Families were often separated at slave auctions.

When owners wanted to buy slaves, they attended auctions. The largest auction took place in Georgia in 1859, where four hundred enslaved people were separated from their loved ones.

were long, so crops were not as plentiful as they were in the South. Instead of working on farms, many Northern slaves worked as servants.

Slaves usually lived in small cabins with dirt floors and were often scarcely fed and barely clothed. They were given one outfit a year, and few slaves were given shoes. Everyone—children, women, men, and the elderly—worked long hours. They had to do the jobs their masters told them to do, and then go home after dark and clean their cabins, sew, cook, or work in their own small gardens.

When slaves in the colonies did something their owners did not approve of, they could be whipped, branded, maimed, or killed. They were treated as property, not as people, and they did not have any rights. Most slaves could not work for someone other than their master without their owner's approval, and they were not permitted to defend themselves against whites. Enslaved people were not allowed to learn how to read or write either, though some of them managed to do so anyway. Lack of freedom, harsh living conditions, and brutality were more than enough reasons to encourage slaves to seek freedom.

From the moment slaves were taken from their communities, they began to resist enslavement. Many fought for their freedom, attacking anyone who tried to capture them. Some of the African men and women who were captured and forced onto crowded, dirty, disease-ridden ships chose to jump overboard or hang themselves rather than be enslaved. Others refused to eat. A few enslaved Africans, such as Joseph Cinqué of the *Amistad*, tried to take over ships and return to their homeland, while still others looked for different ways to escape.

When enslaved Africans arrived in the colonies, they planned revolts, burned down barns, refused to work, and broke tools, all in an effort to resist enslavement. Abolitionists—people who did not believe slavery was right—often helped the enslaved people. It was this type of resistance and determination that gave birth to the Underground Railroad.

Olaudah Equiano

Joseph Cinqué

Twenty-six-year-old Joseph Cinqué, called Sengbe Pieh in Africa, led a revolt in 1839 on a slave ship called the *Amistad*. Researchers believe Cinqué was born in Sierra Leone in West Africa around 1813. Little is known about his personal life, but some sources say he had a wife and children. While in his country, several Africans attacked him and bound him to other captives. They walked to the coast, where Cinqué and other slaves were forced onto a Portuguese slave ship called the *Teçora*. The ship was bound for Havana, Cuba, though it was illegal to trade imported slaves there at that time.

Cinqué and other slaves were eventually sold to two Spanish planters, Don Jose Ruiz and Don Pedro Montez, and ordered onto the *Amistad*. The planters planned to sell the Africans to plantation owners. Their plans were interrupted when Cinqué managed to free himself and the other captives on the ship. Together, they killed the captain and most of the crew.

Cinqué ordered Ruiz and Montez to sail the *Amistad* to Africa. During the day, it seemed as if the two men were taking the Africans back to their homeland, but at night they were secretly heading for the United States. After six weeks at sea, the ship landed near Montauk Point, Long Island, New York. The United States Coast Guard arrested Cinqué and the others. They were charged with mutiny and murder and imprisoned in New Haven, Connecticut.

Abolitionists came to the aid of Cinqué and the others. They raised money, hired lawyers to defend them, and found an interpreter who spoke their language. The Africans went through a trial and several appeals, including one led by former U.S. President John Quincy Adams and held in the U.S. Supreme Court. In 1841, the Supreme Court sided with the Africans and ordered that they be returned to their country.

Slaves on the *Amistad*

Detail from *The Death of Major P...*
1782–1784, painted by John Single...

*Some enslaved people
earned their freedom
by fighting in the
British Army during
the Revolutionary
War. They were
assigned to all-black
regiments, such as the
Royal Ethiopians.*

Freedom Seekers

Though the punishment was tough and the search for freedom was difficult, there were freedom seekers in the colonies before the American Revolution. These freedom seekers could usually go to the homes of free blacks, Native Americans, and some white people for help with traveling underground.

Before 1776, slavery was legal in all the British colonies, so freedom seekers did not view the North as a safe haven. Efforts were made to make escaping difficult. For example, in 1642, Virginia officials declared that all people who helped or hid slaves would be punished. The following year, the New England Confederation—Plymouth Colony, Massachusetts Bay Colony, Connecticut, and New Haven—encouraged its citizens to agree to return runaway slaves to their owners. The agreement did little to stop the flight of slaves.[1] A close look at the laws and rules established during this time reveal that the slaves of colonial America had developed, though unorganized, an underground system of escape.

While colonists from England, accompanied by enslaved Africans, founded Charles Town, Carolina, in 1670, some of the colonies in that area did not belong to the British. There were French, Spanish, and Dutch settlements there as well, but all of them relied on African labor. Shortly after Charles Town was established, enslaved Africans began to outnumber the whites. Taking advantage of their numbers, they resisted slavery by running away. In the early years, slaves in the Carolina colony often ran south to find freedom. In places like St. Augustine, Florida, they could get assistance from British enemies—the Spanish and Native Americans.

Africans helped build Gracia Real de Santa Teresa de Mose, or Fort Mose (MOH-say). This fort, near St. Augustine, became home to nearly 100 Africans who pledged loyalty to the Spanish government.

Although freedom seekers fleeing the Deep South tended to head south, Hudson reports that escapees from Virginia "tended to flee 'north' or 'west' to the often friendly Native American societies living beyond the frontier."[2] Slaves also hid in the swamps, mountains, and unsettled areas, where they formed maroon settlements. Some freedom seekers found help from sympathetic sailors who allowed them to board their ships. By 1726, Virginia had created an act that required ship captains to pledge to "not knowingly or willingly carry or suffer to be carried, in . . . [their] ship[s], any servant or slave that is not attending his or her master or owner, or sent by such master or owner."[3] There are no records to suggest the number of escaped slaves who probably hid on ships with the captain and crew's permission.

A few scholars believe free blacks in South Carolina also served as underground agents. In 1740, South Carolina officials developed a statement that said free blacks who helped runaway slaves would be arrested and sold into slavery to cover the cost of the escaped slave. Though slaves escaped in the North and the South, during this time, escape seemed to be more prevalent among slaves in the South—probably because enslavement was more brutal there. More males than females escaped from North Carolina, Maryland, Virginia, and South Carolina, and more slaves seemed to have escaped from South Carolina than from North Carolina, Maryland, and Virginia.

When slaves ran away, slaveholders tried to locate them. Oftentimes, they relied on flyers and announcements in newspapers, called fugitive slave notices, to let others know their slave was missing. In the *South Carolina Gazette* on October 28, 1732, Robert Hume advertised to try to get others to help him recover his escaped slave:

> RUN away from his Master's Plantation, in the Parish of St. James's Goose Creek, a lusty Negro Man named Hercules, he formerly used to wait on his Master in Charlestown, and is now by Trade a Cooper [barrel maker]. He had on when he went away a blue Duffils Jacket, a pair of ozenbrig Breeches, and speaks very good English. Whoever apprehends and brings him either to the said Plantation in Goose-Creek, or to his Master Robert Hume on Charlestown Neck, shall receive 5 [pounds] . . . besides the usual Allowance for Mileage.[4]

During the Stono Rebellion of 1739, a number of people tried to escape together. Led by Jemmy, a newly arrived slave from Angola, twenty blacks met secretly near the Stono River in South Carolina to plan their escape. The enslaved people had heard that the governor of Florida would grant them freedom. As they marched toward St. Augustine, they took weapons and used military tactics to kill whites. Other blacks joined them until they had increased in number to more than 70 people.

The white Carolinians and the escaped slaves engaged in battle. While some white people died, twice as many escapees were killed. However, a few were said to have escaped into the swamp. Those who were later captured were executed. The rebellion showed that enslaved people were willing to risk their lives fighting for their freedom.

After the rebellion ended, South Carolina's lawmakers created a harsher slave code. "This new code severely limited the privileges of slaves," reports the Library of Congress. "They were no longer allowed to grow their own food,

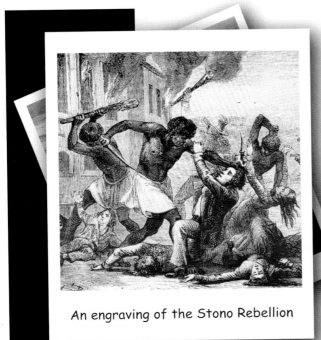

An engraving of the Stono Rebellion

The Stono Rebellion of 1739 took place near Charleston, South Carolina. It was sparked by enslaved people who were determined to get to Florida, because they had heard that the governor there would free escaped slaves.

assemble in groups, earn their own money or learn to read."[5] South Carolina also decided killing an escaped slave was legal. Georgia's laws were also harsh. Georgia officials promised a greater reward to those who returned the dead bodies of adult male escapees to their owners than they offered to those who returned women and children alive.

By the late 1760s, blacks were not the only group in colonial America demanding freedom. Colonists began to get upset with Britain, protesting new laws that were designed to tax them. They did not believe they should pay taxes to help raise money for Britain, and they did not like the way Britain tried to control what they did. Angry, the thirteen colonies went to war against Britain.

Slaves believed that the American Revolution was an important war because it was about obtaining freedom. The first man to die during the war is generally believed to be a fugitive slave named Crispus Attucks, who was killed at the Boston Massacre in 1770. He had lived with his owner in Framingham, Massachusetts, until he ran away—probably in 1750—and became a sailor. An advertisement in the *Boston Gazette* on October 2, 1750, read:

> Ran away from his Master William Brown from Framingham, on the 30th of Sept. last, a Molatto Fellow, about 27 Years of age, named Crispas, 6 Feet two Inches high, short curl'd Hair, his Knees nearer together than common: had on a light colour'd Bearskin Coat. . .[6]

His owner thought he might have hidden on ships because he also wrote, "And all Matters of Vessels and others, are hereby cautioned against concealing [hiding] or carrying off said Servant [Crispus] on Penalty of Law."[7]

Underground attempts to assist enslaved people in escaping became clear to George Washington three years before he was sworn in as the nation's first president. In May of 1786, he discovered one of his own slaves was missing. The slave had escaped from Alexandria, Virginia, to Philadelphia, Pennsylvania, and Washington was sure Quakers had helped him. Washington was not pleased.

Paul Revere's engraving of the Boston Massacre, which took place in 1770. Five colonists, including Crispus Attucks, were killed by British soldiers.

Washington was probably right, because Quakers like Isaac T. Hopper, a member of the Pennsylvania Abolition Society, successfully aided many escapees. Hopper, who lived first in Philadelphia and then in New York after 1829, used his house as a station on the Underground Railroad. He spent most of his life helping blacks. When the Reverend Richard Allen, a free black man from Philadelphia, was arrested by a slave hunter who intended to enslave him, Hopper helped Allen regain his freedom. When Allen was arrested, Hopper paid the legal fees that eventually led to his release. Another time, Hopper put himself in harm's way when a freedom seeker was captured by his owner.

A painting of the Antislavery Society Convention in 1840. Antislavery societies fought against slavery by working on the Underground Railroad and by writing and speaking out against slavery. Members spent most of their lives trying to convince people that slavery was wrong.

Hopper went to the tavern where the owner planned to hold the freedom seeker until they could return to the South. When Hopper tried to help the enslaved man, six guards threw him through a window. Bruised, Hopper still managed to break down the tavern door and rescue the freedom seeker.

Some thought the American Revolution would bring an end to slavery throughout the thirteen colonies, but the luxury of free labor was too great to give up. With each passing year, the colonies had grown more and more dependent on slave labor. For example, the number of blacks in Virginia grew slowly but steadily. While in 1625 there were less than 23 enslaved, in 1650 there were nearly 300, and by 1700, the slave trade was bringing over a thousand Africans to the colony each year.[8] Workers on the Underground Railroad were ready to help them obtain freedom.

FYInfo
FOR YOUR INFORMATION

With Native Americans as their unofficial underground agents, freedom seekers escaped plantations and found refuge in Spanish Florida. The Spaniards had slaves themselves, but they did not view slavery the way Englishman did. In 1686, Spaniards in St. Augustine decided to give religious sanctuary, or refuge, to enslaved people arriving from the English colonies. The following year, the first escaped Africans arrived. They lived with the Spaniards, Native Americans, and free Africans for years.

As the Spanish and British conflict grew, the Spaniards sought protection. They decided to build forts. With the help of Africans and Native Americans, they built Gracia Real de Santa Teresa de Mose (Fort Mose) about two miles from St. Augustine, in 1739.

Fort Mose was one of several forts used to protect Spanish Florida from its enemies. In 1740, English soldiers led by General James Oglethorpe attacked St. Augustine and captured the fort. The people living there reached safety before the English occupied it. The English were eventually defeated, but they destroyed Fort Mose. It took twelve years to build another fort. The people who lived in the first fort moved into the second one and lived there for eleven years. After the French and Indian War in 1763, the Spanish lost Florida to the English. People who had lived in Spanish Florida moved to Cuba.

The second Fort Mose was used by different groups until it was finally destroyed in 1812. Over time, the remains of the first Fort Mose sank as the water level rose in the wetlands. In 1976, Jack Williams found the site of the first Fort Mose on his property. Since 1986, researchers have studied the site. Their findings reveal how the people lived, ate, worked, and defended their land. A traveling exhibit—Fort Mose: Colonial America's Black Fortress of Freedom—opened in 1991. The U.S. Department of the Interior gave Fort Mose national landmark status in 1994.

Fort Mose, near St. Augustine, Florida

Nat Turner, who organized a slave upr[ising was] captured in 1831. Turner was an educo[ted man] who lived in Southampton, Virginia.

In 1831, he and several other men went from house to house and killed every white person they saw. Some of Turner's supporters were arrested, but he managed to get away. He hid for three months before he was discovered in the woods.

Fighting for Freedom

After the Revolutionary War, the colonies began the process of becoming the United States. Officials from the colonies met in 1787 in Philadelphia to write the Constitution. All of them had an opinion about the role of slavery in the newly formed country. George Washington and Thomas Jefferson had slaves, while Benjamin Franklin, Thomas Paine, and John Adams were strongly against slavery. They decided to compromise. Though the authors of the Constitution never used the words *slave* or *slavery*, they decided the slave trade would exist for at least twenty more years.[1] They also decided slaves could not avoid service to their masters by running to a free state or territory.

Northern states began to outlaw slavery, so slaveholders insisted that stiffer laws or rules be created that would allow them to capture a slave who ran into a state that did not allow slavery. The Northwest Ordinance of 1787 was the government's response. It said the land north of the Ohio River—present-day Ohio, Indiana, Illinois, Michigan and Wisconsin—would exclude slavery, but slaves who ran to the Northwest Territory would be returned to their owners.

People soon found out that it is difficult when one part of the country allows slavery and another part does not. What happened when a slave traveled into a part of the country that did not allow slavery? Was the slave to be set free? At the insistence of Southerners, Congress said no. They passed the Fugitive Slave Act of 1793, which said slaves who entered states or territories where slavery was illegal would be arrested and returned to their slaveholding states. The act also stated that any person who assisted a runaway would be fined $500. Though the act seems harsh enough to have stopped enslaved people from escaping or to dissuade their friends from helping, it did not. Instead, enslaved blacks and their allies, or friends, began to put the Underground Railroad in full motion. The number of successful escapes increased.

Sometimes Underground Railroad passengers were creative when planning an escape. Abolitionist William Still wrote, "Occasionally fugitives came in boxes and chests, and not infrequently some were secreted in steamers and vessels, and in some instances journeyed in skiffs. . . . Men disguised in female attire and women dressed in the [clothes] of men have under very trying circumstances triumphed in thus making their way to freedom."[2]

Ellen Craft disguised herself in 1848 when she and her husband escaped from two different plantations in Macon, Georgia. Although Ellen's mother was a slave, her father was her mother's white master, and Ellen's skin looked white. Ellen pretended to be a white male slave owner because women, even white women, rarely traveled alone. When she boarded the train with her husband, who pretended to be her slave, she was wrapped in bandages because she could not read or write and knew she would be asked to sign her name while traveling. With her arm in a sling, she could ask clerks to sign documents for her.

Her husband, William Craft, later wrote in his narrative, *Running a Thousand Miles for Freedom: The Escape of William and Ellen Craft from Slavery* (1860), "Knowing that slaveholders have the privilege of taking their slaves to any part of the country they think proper, it occurred to me that, as my wife was nearly white, I might get her to disguise herself as an invalid gentleman, and assume to be my master."[3] Ellen and William continued their journey on a steamboat and a ferry before arriving eight days later in Philadelphia, where they were helped by William Wells Brown, William Lloyd Garrison, and others.

William Craft wrote, "It is true, our condition as slaves was not by any means the worst; but the mere idea that we were held as [property], and deprived of all legal rights—the thought that we had to give up our hard earnings to a tyrant, to enable him to live in idleness and luxury—the thought that we could not call the bones and sinews that God gave us our own: but above all, the fact that another man had the power to tear from our cradle the new-born babe and sell it . . . and then scourge us if we dared to lift a finger to save it from such a fate, haunted us for years."[4] After he and his wife escaped, William Craft spent many years speaking out against slavery.

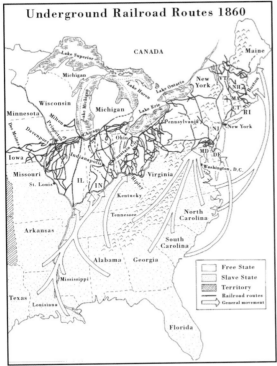

Underground Railroad Routes 1860

For enslaved people headed north, it was easier to escape detection and to navigate by following the natural features of the land. There were several routes along the Mississippi River and the Appalachian Mountains.

    Escaped slaves found unique hiding places when traveling to freedom. When walking through the woods, they were likely to hide in swamps, near rivers and streams, or in barns and stables. They hid in basements. While escaping on boats and trains, some hid among suitcases. Some even traveled in boxes. Probably the most famous person to do this was Henry Brown. Though his owner treated him well, Brown wanted to be free. He wanted his family to be free, too. He had saved money to buy his wife and children, but before he could save enough, his family was sold away. Angry, he decided he had to figure out a way to free himself.

    According to story, as retold by Fergus Bordewich, Brown became "friendly with a white merchant, Samuel Smith, who one day hinted to him . . . that as a man with a valuable trade [as a worker] he might be better off free."[5] Brown admitted that he wanted to be free and asked Smith for advice. Smith and Brown thought of different ideas for escape until Brown decided he would hide in a box and ask someone to mail him to a free state. "Smith managed to send a message to the Philadelphia Anti-Slavery Office, advising it to watch

The Resurrection of Henry Brown, 1850, Samuel W. Rowse. Brown was one of many freedom seekers who were shipped to free states in boxes or crates.

for a crate that would be arriving on a certain date, and to open it immediately."[6]

Brown asked a free black man to make the box for him. The box was "three feet long, two feet wide, and two feet, six inches deep. . . . The fit would be tight, allowing the two-hundred-pound five-foot-eight-inch-tall Brown no space to turn himself around."[7] Three holes were drilled into the box so that Brown would have air. Before getting into the box, he was given food and water for the journey. Smith took the box to a railway office in Richmond, Virginia, and Brown was finally headed for freedom. The trip was difficult—he banged his head several times—but he reached Philadelphia safely after nearly twenty-seven hours of travel. He was taken to the house of abolitionist Lucretia Mott, where her family welcomed him. Smith, however, wasn't so lucky. In 1848, he went to jail for eight years for boxing and shipping two other escapees.[8]

With the help of the Underground Railroad, escaped slaves managed to find freedom in different places. Some freedom seekers traveled by boat to some of the Sea Islands off the coast of South Carolina, Georgia, and northern Florida, where they settled. Some escapees joined the gold rush in California. Others helped settle the Kansas territory. Freedom seekers built communities in Canada, too. Still others went to gold fields as far away from the United States as Australia, and some found freedom in Britain. Wherever freedom seekers settled, they usually found jobs and homes where they could start families. A number of escaped slaves became abolitionists, settling in Massachusetts, New York, and Connecticut.

Philadelphia was an important city for the Underground Railroad. When the city was founded in 1682 by William Penn, a Quaker, slavery was legal. According to Underground Railroad scholar J. Blaine Hudson, by 1730, "about 4,000 enslaved African Americans were residents in Pennsylvania . . . and this number increased to roughly 10,000 by 1790."[9]

During the antebellum period, numerous freedom seekers traveling on the Underground Railroad stopped in Philadelphia for help from white and black abolitionists. Philadelphia had strong abolitionist groups and vigilance committees. A few famous passengers who arrived in Philadelphia include Henry "Box" Brown and William and Ellen Craft. Some of the more famous of the agents and conductors of the railroad lived in or near Philadelphia,

Frances Ellen Watkins Harper

too. Lucretia Mott, William Still, Thomas Garrett, and Harriet Tubman are a few.

Robert Purvis, a member of the Philadelphia Underground Railroad and the Philadelphia Vigilance Committee, used his mother's house to harbor, or hide, freedom seekers. The house had a trapdoor that led to a secret room in the basement. When Purvis moved to another home, he also used it as a station. Although he never used his last home to harbor escaped slaves, a Pennsylvania Historical and Museum Commission marker was placed there to honor him.

Frances Ellen Watkins Harper, an antislavery poet, teacher, lecturer, and activist, also used her home as a safe harbor for escaped slaves. Harper was born free in Maryland, but she left the area to teach in Columbus, Ohio. After a brief stay there, she moved to Pennsylvania and began giving speeches and writing poetry, such as "The Slave Mother" and "Bury Me in a Free Land," to let people know about the horrific conditions of slavery. The work of the Underground Railroad was expensive. Escaped slaves and the people who helped them needed to have access to food, clothes, legal help, and transportation. As a stockholder, Harper donated money from the sale of her books to help pay for the efforts of the Underground Railroad.

Two fugitive slaves rest in front of a
Virginia in 1863. Some slaves fought for
during the Civil War (1861–1865).

*Fugitive slaves usually
slept during the day
and traveled at night
because they did not
want anyone to see
them. They knew that
if they were caught,
they would be
punished and taken
back to their owners.*

Final Stop

Throughout the years, thousands of freedom seekers left Southern plantations via the Underground Railroad. As their escapes became clear, owners grew angry. Southerners had threatened for some time to leave the Union, and over the years the government had tried to compromise. After the Mexican-American War ended with the Treaty of Guadalupe in 1848, the nation tried to decide what it would do with the new land it had won. Would slavery be allowed in the territory? Abolitionists said no, but slaveholders shouted yes. There was also the problem concerning California. California wanted to enter the Union as a free state. If that happened, the number of free and slave states would no longer be balanced. In the end, California was admitted into the Union as a free state, and Congress decided to leave it up to the leaders in the new territory—present-day New Mexico, Nevada, Arizona, and Utah—to decide if they would allow slavery.

Slaveholders were not too happy with the compromise. They argued that Congress needed to develop a tougher law that would help ensure the return of their slaves. In response, the Fugitive Slave Act of 1850 was introduced as a part of the Compromise of 1850. This Fugitive Slave Act required citizens to help capture and return fugitive slaves, and it denied a fugitive's right to a jury trial. Slave catchers were allowed to capture slaves in states that did not support slavery. They would patrol the streets at night, looking for escapees. An escaped slave named Anthony Burns was one of the many who were captured and returned to slavery. Burns had escaped from Virginia. In 1854 he was arrested in Boston, Massachusetts, and eventually returned to his owner. (He was later set free when abolitionists raised enough money to buy his freedom; he returned to Boston in 1855.) Sometimes when slave catchers did not find escapees, they would kidnap free blacks. Finding themselves in danger too, many free blacks left the United States and settled in Canada.

Although escaped slaves and those who helped them were left with fewer options, they did not stop working on the Underground Railroad. In fact, it seemed their efforts to help escapees increased. Throughout the nation, many people who hadn't concerned themselves with the issue of slavery were now set against it. Christian abolitionists believed it was their duty to help freedom seekers because they believed in passages from the Bible that said it was the Christian thing to do. In Deuteronomy, chapter 23, it says:

> Thou shalt not deliver unto his master the servant which is escaped from his master unto thee; He shall dwell with thee, [even] among you, in that place which he shall choose in one of thy gates, where it liketh him best: thou shalt not oppress him.[1]

Instead of settling in the Northern area of the United States, freedom seekers after 1850 were more likely to travel to Canada. Canadians did not have fugitive slave laws, and escapees found support in places such as Niagara Falls, Hamilton, and Windsor. Freedom seekers built churches, towns, businesses, and schools. Mary Ann Shadd was one of the free blacks who left the United States to settle in Canada. She also traveled around the United States to encourage blacks to move to Canada. It is said that about 20,000 blacks moved there.[2] Shadd's father, Abraham Shadd, had served as a conductor on the Underground Railroad while Mary Ann was growing up in West Chester, Pennsylvania. In Canada, she and her family continued to help escaped slaves, and she opened a school for blacks. In 1856, she married Thomas F. Cary and became known as Mary Ann Shadd Cary.

Tension increased between the North and South. Some Southerners were angry because some Northerners routinely broke laws concerning assisting and harboring slaves. Many Northerners were angry because Southerners were given the right to come into their cities and arrest freedom seekers. For over ten years, Southerners and Northerners argued. Finally, in December 1860, South Carolina seceded, or withdrew, from the Union. This means South Carolina decided it would no longer be a part of the United States. Other Southern

CAUTION!!

COLORED PEOPLE

OF BOSTON, ONE & ALL,

You are hereby respectfully CAUTIONED and
advised, to avoid conversing with the

Watchmen and Police Officers of Boston,

For since the recent ORDER OF THE MAYOR &
ALDERMEN, they are empowered to act as

KIDNAPPERS
AND
Slave Catchers,

And they have already been actually employed in
KIDNAPPING, CATCHING, AND KEEPING
SLAVES. Therefore, if you value your LIBERTY,
and the *Welfare of the Fugitives* among you, *Shun*
them in every possible manner, as so many *HOUNDS*
on the track of the most unfortunate of your race.

Keep a Sharp Look Out for KIDNAPPERS, and have TOP EYE open.

APRIL 24, 1851.

states such as Mississippi, Florida, Alabama, and Georgia followed in 1861. The nation was divided. The Southern states eventually created a Congress, declared themselves the Confederate States of America, and elected Jefferson Davis of Mississippi as their president. The Civil War began on April 12, 1861.

The Northern states were defended by the Union army, and the Southern states raised the Confederate army. Just as they did during the American Revolution, freedom seekers used the Civil War as an opportunity to escape from slavery. Frederick Douglass encouraged Abraham Lincoln to allow blacks to fight in the war. Lincoln agreed, and people such as Mary Shadd Cary recruited black soldiers for the Union army. Harriet Tubman served as a nurse and a spy during the war.

Abolitionists wanted President Lincoln to end slavery. Lincoln said emancipation, or freedom for enslaved people, should be slow. There were still four slave states—Delaware, Maryland, Kentucky, and Missouri—in the Union, and Lincoln did not want to anger them. He decided to free the slaves in the Confederate states. He read the Emancipation Proclamation, which freed the slaves in the Confederate states, in 1862, and it became law on January 1, 1863.

Although the Emancipation Proclamation is cited as the first step to free the slaves in the United States, it did not free them in Delaware, Maryland, Kentucky, or Missouri. It also did not really free the slaves in Confederate states, since those states did not recognize Lincoln as their president.

The war ended in 1865 when the Confederate states surrendered. The North had won, and the Union was restored. On January 31, 1865, Congress had passed the Thirteenth Amendment of the United States Constitution. It ended slavery, declaring, "Neither slavery nor involuntary servitude . . . shall exist within the United States."[3] The amendment was approved by the states on December 6, 1865. With slavery abolished, the Underground Railroad was no longer needed.

Since slavery was over, agents, conductors, and station masters could begin to share some of the secrets and signals of the Underground Railroad. As corresponding secretary of the Vigilance Committee of the Philadelphia Anti-Slavery Society, William Still recorded information about their work. He had been an agent and conductor on the Underground Railroad who helped

William Still, 1872

Still's parents were slaves, but they escaped before he was born. While working as an abolitionist, Still met a freedom seeker named Peter Still. He realized that Peter was his brother, the child his mother had to leave in slavery when she ran away.

numerous escapees. According to some researchers, "19 out of every 20 fugitive slaves passing through Philadelphia stopped at his house."[4] Still's recorded notes begin with work done after 1851, though the committee began working to help freedom seekers in 1835. Still hid his notes about freedom seekers, he said, "in the attic of the Lebanon Seminary and in a graveyard."[5] In 1872, he published the information in a book titled *The Underground Railroad*. In the beginning of the book, he wrote, "In these Records will be found interesting narratives of the escapes of many men, women and children, from the prison-house of bondage. . . . Not a few, upon arriving, of course, hardly had rags enough on them to cover their nakedness, even in the coldest weather. . . . They were determined to have liberty even at the cost of life."[6]

A few years later another prominent worker on the Underground Railroad published a book: *Reminiscences of Levi Coffin, the Reputed President of the Underground Railroad* (1876). Coffin had kept a diary for most of his life. He used it and other documents he had to tell what he knew about freedom seekers and the people who helped them.

Many of the stations on the Underground Railroad became national landmarks. William Still's house was razed in 1992, but a Pennsylvania Historical and Museum Commission marker shows where it once stood. Levi and Catherine Coffin's home, called the "Grand Central Station of the Underground Railroad," is now a historic site in Indiana.[7] There are other registered historical sites—homes, churches, YMCAs, and offices—that mark Underground Railroad stops in different parts of the United States.

The Underground Railroad made its last stop during the Civil War, but it should never be forgotten. On November 28, 1990, Congress enacted a law that directed the National Park Service to commemorate the Underground Railroad. Congress wanted scholars to be able to locate and study sites on the Underground Railroad so that future generations could learn about the people who owned and visited them.

In 2000, President William Jefferson Clinton signed the National Underground Railroad Freedom Center Act. The act provided $16 million to help maintain Underground Railroad sites throughout the United States and to develop museums and educational programs at those sites. These would help keep the memory of its courageous passengers and agents, generous stockholders, and sites alive.

The National Underground Railroad Freedom Center, in Cincinnati, Ohio, opened to the public in August 2004.

The Fugitive Slave Act of 1850 made it easier for slave owners to search for escaped slaves. Many were found and arrested. Anthony Burns was one of them. He had escaped on a boat in 1854 from his owner, Charles F. Suttle, of Alexandria, Virginia. Once Burns reached Boston, Massachusetts, he found a job in a clothing store. Asa O. Butman, a man who made his living looking for escaped slaves, entered the clothing store and saw Burns. On May 24, Butman had Burns arrested and taken to the Boston Courthouse.

After Burns was arrested, black and white abolitionists, including William Lloyd Garrison, Wendell Phillips, and Thomas Higginson, protested. They marched to the Boston Courthouse and tried to free Burns. When deputies tried to stop them, they fought and injured one of the deputies. The deputy died later. Historians called the fight "The Boston Riot." Abolitionists, led by Reverend Leonard A. Grimes, raised enough money to buy Burns's freedom, but they were not allowed to make the purchase. U.S. law enforcers wanted to carry out the Fugitive Slave Act, and they did not want abolitionists to stand in their way.

Burns was not given any rights. He was not allowed bail, to have a jury at his trial, or to testify on his behalf. On June 2, 1854, when Burns was led to the ship that would take him back to slavery, nearly two thousand soldiers escorted him to it while 50,000 people watched.

The abolitionists managed to purchase Burns' freedom after he was returned to Virginia. He became an antislavery speaker for a while and eventually moved to St. Catherine's, Ontario, Canada.[8]

Anthony Burns and Thomas Sims are escorted through Boston to be returned to bondage. Sims was actually returned three years before Burns.

Chronology

1441 Portugal begins slave trade with West Africa.

1581 Spaniards bring Africans to their colony in St. Augustine, Florida.

1619 The first Africans arrive in the British colonies. They land in Virginia.

1640 Massachusetts Bay becomes the first British colony to legalize slavery.

1641 John Punch, an African indentured servant, is sentenced to servitude for life for running away.

1642 Virginia laws say it is illegal to help enslaved people who run away.

1688 Members of the Society of Friends, or Quakers, agree to protest slavery.

1705 Virginia laws allow slaveholders to kill enslaved people who runaway.

1739 The Stono Rebellion takes place in South Carolina. Gracia Real de Santa Teresa de Mose (Fort Mose) is established for African Americans near St. Augustine, Florida.

1740 North Carolina passes a law that makes it illegal to help enslaved people run away.

1763 British take possession of Spanish Florida. People living in Florida resettle in Cuba.

1770 Crispus Attucks, a fugitive slave, is the first to die during the American Revolution.

1775 The Revolutionary War begins. The Pennsylvania Abolition Society is created to help fugitive slaves.

1776 The Declaration of Independence is signed.

1777 Vermont bans slavery. Other Northern states follow.

1783 The American Revolution ends.

1786 George Washington claims that Quakers helped his slave escape.

1787 The Northwest Ordinance says slavery will not exist in what will become Ohio, Indiana, Illinois, Michigan and Wisconsin. Isaac T. Hopper begins helping fugitive slaves.

1793 The first Fugitive Slave Act says slave owners can go into other states to capture enslaved people.

1804 General Thomas Boudes of Columbia, Pennsylvania, refuses to give a fugitive slave to law enforcers.

1826 Levi Coffin is known as the President of the Underground Railroad.

1831 William Lloyd Garrison founds *The Liberator*, an abolitionist newspaper.

1838 Frederick Douglass escapes slavery.

1843 Sojourner Truth begins her work as an abolitionist.

1849 Harriet Tubman escapes slavery, but she returns repeatedly to lead other enslaved people to freedom.

1850 Fugitive Slave Law passes.

1860 Abraham Lincoln is elected president. South Carolina leaves the Union.

1861 Civil War begins.

1863 Abraham Lincoln signs the Emancipation Proclamation.

1865 Civil War ends. The Thirteenth Amendment says slavery is illegal.

1868 The Fourteenth Amendment secures citizenship rights for all Americans, including African Americans.

1877 Reconstruction ends.

1909 The National Association for the Advancement of Colored People (NAACP) is organized.

1929 Civil rights leader Dr. Martin Luther King Jr. is born.

1954 In *Brown v. Board of Education of Topeka, Kansas*, the Supreme Court says students of different races can go to school together.

1955 Montgomery Bus Boycott begins in Montgomery, Alabama.

1957 Nine students integrate Central High School in Little Rock, Arkansas.

1963 Dr. King gives his "I Have a Dream" speech at the March on Washington for Jobs and Freedom in Washington, D.C.

1964 President Lyndon B. Johnson signs the Civil Rights Act of 1964.

1967 Thurgood Marshall becomes the first African American Supreme Court Justice.

1990 Congress enacts a law that allows for the study of sites connected to the Underground Railroad.

1991 Clarence Thomas becomes the second African American Supreme Court Justice.

1992 Astronaut Mae Jemison is the first African American woman in space.

1994 Fort Mose is given national landmark status.

2000 President William Jefferson Clinton signs the National Underground Railroad Freedom Center Act.

2004 The 50th anniversary of *Brown v. Board of Education of Topeka, Kansas*, is celebrated.

2006 Ceremonial groundbreaking takes place on the National Mall for the Dr. Martin Luther King, Jr., Memorial.

2007 Jamestown, Virginia, celebrates its 400th anniversary.

2009 African American Barack Obama becomes the 44th U.S. president.

Chapter Notes

Chapter 1. Running the Railroad

1. George Hendrick and Willene Hendrick, ed., *Fleeing for Freedom: Stories of the Underground Railroad, As Told by Levi Coffin and William Still* (Chicago: Ivan R. Dee, 2004), p. 3.

2. J. Blaine Hudson, *Encyclopedia of the Underground Railroad* (Jefferson, NC: McFarland, 2006), p. 162.

3. Fergus M. Bordewich, *Bound for Canaan: The Underground Railroad and the War for the Soul of America* (New York: Amistad, 2005), p. 235.

4. Susan Michaels, *Underground Railroad*, DVD (New York: History Channel, 2002).

5. Bordewich, p. 356.

6. Jacqueline Tobin and Raymond G. Dobard, *Hidden in Plain View: The Secret Story of Quilts and the Underground Railroad* (New York: Doubleday, 1999), p. 64.

7. Hendrick and Hendrick, p. 4.

8. Hudson, p. 2.

9. Ibid., pp. 1–2.

Chapter 2. A Slave for Life

1. Lisa Gensheimer, *Safe Harbor*, DVD (North East, PA: Main Street Media, 2003).

2. Fergus M. Bordewich, *Bound for Canaan: The Underground Railroad and the War for the Soul of America* (New York: Amistad, 2005), p. 15.

3. Lerone Bennett Jr., *Before the Mayflower: A History of Black America*, 7th ed. (Chicago: Johnson, 1982), p. 45.

4. Arna Bontemps, ed. *Great Slave Narratives* (Boston: Beacon Press, 1969), pp. 19–20.

5. Susan Altman, *The Encyclopedia of African-American Heritage* (New York: Facts on File, Inc., 1997), p. 225.

Chapter 3. Freedom Seekers

1. George Hendrick and Willene Hendrick, eds., *Fleeing for Freedom: Stories of the Underground Railroad, As Told by Levi Coffin and William Still* (Chicago: Ivan R. Dee, 2004), p. 5.

2. J. Blaine Hudson, *Encyclopedia of the Underground Railroad* (Jefferson, NC: McFarland, 2006), p. 1.

3. E. Delorus Preston, "The Genesis of the Underground Railroad," *The Journal of Negro History*, 18.2, 1933, p. 149.

4. "Runaway Notices," http://www.pbs.org/wgbh/aia/part1/1h309t.html.

5. "Stono's Rebellion," http://www.americaslibrary.gov/cgi-bin/page.cgi/jb/colonial/stono_2

6. "Crispus Attucks," http://www.pbs.org/wgbh/aia/part2/2p24.html.

7. Ibid.

8. Lerone Bennett, Jr., *Before the Mayflower: A History of Black America*, 7th ed. (Chicago: Johnson, 1982), p. 46.

Chapter 4. Fighting for Freedom

1. J. Blaine Hudson, *Encyclopedia of the Underground Railroad* (Jefferson, NC: McFarland, 2006), p. 27.

2. William Still, *The Underground Railroad* (Chicago: Johnson Publishing, 1872), p. xi.

3. Arna Bontemps, ed. *Great Slave Narratives* (Boston: Beacon Press, 1969), p. 286.

4. Ibid., p. 271.

5. Fergus M. Bordewich, *Bound for Canaan: The Underground Railroad and the War for the Soul of America* (New York: Amistad, 2005), p. 310.

6. Ibid.

7. Ibid.

8. Still, p. 71.

9. Hudson, p. 165.

Chapter 5. Final Stop

1. Deuteronomy 23: 15–16, King James Version, on the Internet at http://www.godrules.net/library/kjv/kjvdeu23.htm

2. Fergus M. Bordewich, *Bound for Canaan: The Underground Railroad and the War for the Soul of America* (New York: Amistad, 2005), p. 379.

3. "Primary Documents in American History," http://www.loc.gov/rr/program/bib/ourdocs/13thamendment.html

4. Charles L. Blockson, *Hippocrene Guide to the Underground Railroad* (New York: Hippocrene Books, 1994), p. 84.

5. George Hendrick and Willene Hendrick, ed., *Fleeing for Freedom: Stories of the Underground Railroad, As Told by Levi Coffin and William Still* (Chicago: Ivan R. Dee, 2004), p. 17.

6. William Still, *The Underground Railroad* (Chicago: Johnson Publishing, 1872), p. vii.

7. Blockson, p. 229.

8. "Anthony Burns Captured." http://www.pbs.org/wgbh/aia/part4/4p2915.html

Further Reading

For Young Adults

Cary, Lorene. *Free: Great Escapes from Slavery on the Underground Railroad.* Chicago: Third World Press, 2006.

Eskridge, Ann E. *Slave Uprisings and Runaways: Fighting for Freedom and the Underground Railroad* (Slavery in American History). Berkeley Heights, NJ: Enslow, 2004.

Wolney, Philip. *The Underground Railroad: A Primary Source History of the Journey to Freedom.* New York: Rosen, 2009.

Works Consulted

African American Community of Freedom
http://www.fortmose.org/

African Americans at Jamestown
http://www.nps.gov/jame/historyculture/african-americans-at-jamestown.htm

Altman, Susan. *The Encyclopedia of African-American Heritage.* New York: Facts on File, Inc., 1997.

"Anthony Burns: A History." http://docsouth.unc.edu/neh/stevens/stevens.html

"Anthony Burns Captured." http://www. pbs.org/wgbh/aia/part4/4p2915.html

Bennett, Lerone, Jr. *Before the Mayflower: A History of Black America*, 7th ed. Chicago: Johnson, 1982.

Blockson, Charles L. *Hippocrene Guide to the Underground Railroad*. New York: Hippocrene Books, 1994.

Bontemps, Arna, ed. *Great Slave Narratives*. Boston: Beacon Press, 1969.

Bordewich, Fergus M. *Bound for Canaan: The Underground Railroad and the War for the Soul of America*. New York: Amistad, 2005.

"The Compromise of 1850 and the Fugitive Slave Act." http://www.pbs. org/wgbh/aia/part4/4p2951.html

"Crispus Attucks." http://www.pbs.org/ wgbh/aia/part2/2p24.html

Gensheimer, Lisa. *Safe Harbor*. DVD. North East, PA: Main Street Media, 2003.

Hendrick, George, and Willene Hendrick, eds. *Fleeing for Freedom: Stories of the Underground Railroad, As Told by Levi Coffin and William Still*. Chicago: Ivan R. Dee, 2004.

Hudson, J. Blaine. *Encyclopedia of the Underground Railroad*. Jefferson, NC: McFarland, 2006.

Holy Bible, King James Version.

Michaels, Susan. *Underground Railroad*. DVD. New York: History Channel, 2002.

"National Underground Railroad Freedom Center Act." http://www. cbo.gov/doc. cfm?index=2529&type=0

Preston, E. Delorus. "The Genesis of the Underground Railroad." *The Journal of Negro History*. Volume 18.2, 144-170, 1933.

"Primary Documents in American History." http://www.loc.gov/rr/ program/bib/ourdocs/ 13thamendment.html

Reminiscences of Levi Coffin, the Reputed President of the Underground Railroad. Cincinnati, Ohio: Western Tract Society, 1876. Retrieved from Internet Archive on November 28, 2008: http://www. archive.org/stream/ reminiscencesof100coff

"Runaways." http://www.pbs.org/wgbh/ aia/part2/2p17.html

"Runaway Notices." http://www.pbs. org/wgbh/aia/part1/1h309t.html

Still, William. *The Underground Railroad: A Record of Facts, Authentic Narratives, Letters, & C., Narrating the Hardships, Hair-Breadth Escapes and Death Struggles of the Slaves in Their Efforts for Freedom, as Related by Themselves and Others, or Witnessed by the Author*. Chicago: Johnson Publishing, 1872.

"Stono's Rebellion." http://www. americaslibrary.gov/cgi-bin/page. cgi/jb/colonial/stono_2

"Text of the Northwest Ordinance." http://www.earlyamerica.com/ earlyamerica/milestones/ordinance/ text.html

Tobin, Jacqueline, and Raymond G. Dobard. *Hidden in Plain View: The Secret Story of Quilts and the Underground Railroad*. New York: Doubleday, 1999.

"Underground Railroad: Special Resource Study." http://www.nps. gov/undergroundrr/purpose.htm

"What Was the Underground Railroad?" http://education.ucdavis.edu/NEW/STC/lesson/socstud/railroad/Whatis.htm

Fugitive slaves carried oil-fueled lanterns while traveling at night.

On the Internet
Aboard the Underground Railroad
   http://www.nps.gov/history/Nr/travel/underground/
National Underground Railroad Freedom Center
   http://www.freedomcenter.org/
The Underground Railroad
   http://www.nationalgeographic.com/railroad/j1.html
Whispers of Angels
   http://www.whispersofangels.com/index.html

Glossary

abolish (uh-BAH-lish)—To end something that has existed for a long time.

abolitionist (aa-buh-LIH-shuh-nist)—Someone who wants to end a law.

ambivalent (am-BIH-vuh-lunt)—Someone who is unsure about how they feel about something or someone.

antebellum (an-tuh-BEL-um)—Existing before a war; particularly, before the Civil War.

brutality (broo-TAL-ih-tee)—Being cruel or mean.

convicted (kun-VIK-ted)—Found guilty of a crime.

fugitive (FYOO-jih-tiv)—Someone who runs away.

maroon (muh-ROON)—To live in a deserted area alone.

mutiny (MYOOT-nee)—To attack or rebel against the captain and officers of a ship.

ozenbrig breeches (OH-zin-brig BRIH-chez)—Pants made out of cotton.

Quaker (KWAY-ker)—A member of the Society of Friends, a religious group that opposes war.

refuge (REF-yooj)—Shelter or protection.

skiff—A small, flat-bottomed rowboat.

Index